ARIES

ARIES

Let your Sun sign show you the way
to a happy and fulfilling life

Marion Williamson & Pam Carruthers

ARCTURUS

ARCTURUS

This edition published in 2021 by Arcturus Publishing
Limited
26/27 Bickels Yard, 151–153 Bermondsey Street,
London SE1 3HA

ISBN: 978-1-83940-139-8
AD008737UK

Printed in China

CONTENTS

Introduction

*W*elcome, Aries! You have just taken a step towards what might become a lifelong passion. When astrology gets under your skin, there's no going back. Astrology helps you understand yourself and the people around you, and its dazzling insights become more fascinating the deeper you go.

Just as the first humans turned to the life-giving Sun for sustenance and guidance, your astrological journey begins with your Sun sign of Aries. First, we delve deeply into the heart of what makes you tick, then we'll continue to unlock your cosmic potential by exploring love, your career and health, where you might prefer to live, and how you get along with family and friends.

Then it's over to gifted astrologer, Pam Carruthers, for her phenomenal birthdate analysis, where she gives personality insights for every single specific Aries birthday.

In the last part of the book we get right inside how astrology works by revealing the different layers that will help you understand your own birth chart and offer the planetary tools to get you started.

Are you ready Aries? Of course you are – you were born ready!

CUSP DATES FOR ARIES
21 March – 20 April

The exact time of the Sun's entry into each zodiac sign varies every year, so it's impossible to list them all. If you were born a day either side of the dates above, you're a 'cusp' baby. This means you may feel like you're a blend of Aries/Pisces or Aries/Taurus, or you may instinctively just know that you're one sign right to your core.

Going deeper

If you want to know once and for all whether you're a Pisces, Aries or Taurus, you can look up your birthdate in a planetary ephemeris, of which there are plenty online. (See page 102 for more information.) This shows the exact moment the Sun moved into a new zodiac sign for the month you were born.

The Aries personality

*Y*ou are a passionate Fire sign ruled by action-oriented, take-no-prisoners Mars. Fire Sun signs are usually forthright, energetic and creative with an unrivalled lust for life. As the first sign of the zodiac, you are a natural leader, a pioneering go-getter who lets nothing get in your way. You like to be first and you play to win. You accomplish your goals fast, fearlessly and furiously, and, yes, you may run out of steam a little towards the end of more complicated projects. But the momentum with which you propel everything you do, is usually powerful enough to cover all the important stuff. Maybe best let a more detail-oriented sign like Virgo or Capricorn, tie up the loose ends.

LET'S GO!

You prefer taking action rather than talking or thinking, and the more challenging a problem the higher its value seems to you. Your reactions are lightning fast, and you instinctively understand how to make things happen. This can make you a little impatient with more considerate types who like to weigh up pros and cons. Your natural assertiveness fires you up to get moving without delay – why would anyone want to waste time discussing the details? You have stuff to do and there's fun to be had!

You're not one to dwell in the past or to overthink yourself into a corner. Leave all that introspection to the Water signs. You prefer to go it alone and act independently as it means you don't have to wait about for anyone else, besides just one of you is quicker than any team of experts. The results may sometimes be a little rough around the edges – but the job gets done.

Your uncomplicated approach to life means you prefer to take things at face value, and if snags arise further down the line, you'll cross those bridges when you come to them. But instead what tends to happen is that you lose a bit of interest when things run into boring problems such as waiting for other people to make decisions, funding problems or being told you're being unrealistic. When things slow down, you're often tempted to begin a new exciting plan, which seems more fun … until you run into similar, energy-sapping, obstacles.

Give yourself time before you agree to something you won't really be able to give your full attention. The same can be said about your romantic relationships, too. Many Aries get married early in a flush of excitement, wishing they'd given things a bit more time at the start to make sure they were really compatible.

MONEY TO BURN

Cash comes in as fast as it goes out in your world. If you're living in the fast lane, you need your money to be there for the spending. Saving is an alien concept because, for you, money in the bank is just an adventure waiting to happen. You're an impulsive spender and if you see something that makes you happy right now, why would you deny yourself? You're the splurge master, spending everything on a fabulous weekend then living on breakfast cereal for the rest of the month. You learn about money the hard way, by kicking yourself every time you max out your credit cards or having to find money that just isn't there to pay the bills. Maybe don't keep your favourite shopping sites on your phone, because impulse buying is not your friend!

TRAILBLAZER

You're a very energetic, physical person, which has probably taken its toll on your joints over the years. Your daring antics in your younger years will have a left more than their fair share of scrapes and bruises, but you wear your battle scars proudly. As far as you're concerned, the aim is not to get to the end in perfect condition, the plan is to have lived life as fully and intensely as possible. Though trailblazing your way through life inevitably means you'll run out of energy eventually. You prefer to charge in, all guns blazing, do your thing and leave, which is great for dramatic effect, but not so impressive for tasks that require patience and stamina – or are in any way boring! Paperwork, household chores and other necessary, but dull, activities tend to get left until they threaten to bury you completely. *Or*, when you can afford to, you just pay someone else to get on with it. Your world needs to be filled with excitement and adventure for you to feel fulfilled. But you're also excellent at creating your own goals and motivating others to smash through theirs, too.

BRAVE HEART

Your courage is legendary and that applies to matters of the heart as well as your physical prowess. You're not frightened to speak out about how you feel and because you're more inclined to extrovert tendencies, you usually find it quite cathartic to express your emotions freely. You accept your feelings readily without prejudice or analysis – you feel what you feel – and that's all there is to it! As a Mars-ruled individual, anger can sometimes boil up to the surface and you're no stranger to a good old-fashioned tantrum. But thanks to your emotional openness, your frustration tends to be explosive, short-lived and quickly forgotten. But explain that to the mild-mannered Piscean whose hair stood on end when you scolded them for not holding the elevator!

Where others fear to speak, you say exactly what's on your mind. You may have a reputation for being a little tactless or abrupt, but you're also admired for your wonderfully outspoken nature. You don't usually set out to intentionally offend anyone, but if you do say something out of turn, you'll not dwell on the consequences too much. More inward-looking Sun signs might gasp in awe at the apparent ease you brush off misunderstandings, but you don't place too much importance on chit-chat. You say what most people are thinking, and secretly wish that everyone else would do the same. The world would certainly be a less complicated place if everyone were an Aries!

RAM OR SHEEP?

Your feisty bluntness can have other people thinking you're a tougher cookie than you actually are. But because you're so open and honest with others, you're genuinely stung when people you know well resort to underhand or manipulative tactics to get back at you in some way.

It's not in you to be scheming or devious – you wear your heart on your sleeve. You yell, you stamp your feet – you may even stick pins in a few voodoo dolls, but then it's over. You worked through it. So, discovering that other people have been plotting against you can come as quite a shock.

Handling other people's frustration and anger is certainly a life lesson you'll encounter – or will have now mastered. But you're hurt to the core if you discover you've been lied to. In a way you'd rather people just got plain angry or punched you, because then you'd know what you were dealing with. Honesty is your superpower, so to have it used against you, can leave you feeling bewildered.

If wounded, you'll put on a brave face but will need plenty of alone time to piece yourself together.

Unfortunately, not everyone is as confident in themselves as you are, so you may rub more introspective types up the wrong way, occasionally. Luckily though, you're not usually a brooder, and recover relatively quickly from any setbacks.

LIBRA LESSON

Your opposite sign of Libra knows a thing or two about balance and co-operation, which aren't always your strongest points. Fellow Librans teach you to work with others, rather than just storming ahead on your own, and doing whatever you assume others want. The Libran way is to ask how they can help – and to really pay attention to the answers!

Librans can be indecisive, but you can learn from their more nuanced approach that every situation has two sides. This relationship-oriented sign understands that diplomacy and tact can also get you where you need to go in life – and not everything needs to be a battle.

Your positive approach keeps your energy fresh, vibrant and pure. But slow down a little before you dive into the deep end. Smell the roses and, you, know, think things through before committing. Nobody could accuse you of sitting on the fence, but maybe you could straddle it now and then, and talk to the people on each side. When you take other people's opinions and ideas on board, you become an unstoppable, Fire-powered force for good!

YOU'LL NOT REGRET ANYTHING YOU'VE DONE – IT'S THE THINGS YOU DON'T DO THAT WILL TORMENT YOU.

Aries in love

*Y*ou love with a childlike, uncomplicated joy. You don't have the patience for mind games and rarely waste time on somebody who cannot return your affections. You're open and honest about your feelings and not subtle, which can be a little unnerving! But your uncomplicated approach makes you a refreshing, exciting person to be in love with. You can be a bit bossy at times, but your partner doesn't see this at first because they're so caught up in your ardent, blinding affection. You need a strong other half who can match your energy and who won't be afraid of a challenge.

INSTANT ATTRACTION

You will have had more than your fair share of experiences of love at first sight, after all, you are the first sign of the zodiac and first impressions mean a great deal to you. You fall hard and fast with a burning desire and you're usually the one who initiates contact. You're not backwards in coming forwards and have a knack for knowing how to impress the person you have your heart set on. As you're not scared to approach people you like, you may have many love relationships in your life before settling on someone special. You have complete faith in yourself, but you take a while to feel that sure about anyone else.

As an energetic Fire sign your sex appeal is obvious, though the intense heat can cool quickly if your lover has a lazy streak or seems to be a bit of a pushover. When you decide you really care about someone, you call off the attack dogs, and your chosen person will discover a very romantic soul that loves with the uncomplicated innocence of a child.

CARING – YES. SHARING? – HMMM

Even in your closest relationships you're an independent free spirit so sharing your life with someone else can feel a little daunting. Cooking for another can feel like a big deal at first – never mind having to share your living space and time. But if your mate understands and is willing for you to take charge, there won't be too many shouting matches. Though if your partner begins to get too clingy you may have to have an adult conversation.

TRICKY EMOTIONS

You hate feeling vulnerable; only a few carefully chosen people ever really get to see the trusting little child in you. But when you feel safe and loved, you let your guard down completely. Your confidence in others' love is hard won, so if you feel taken for granted or disappointed in your partner, it can be devastating. A little naively sometimes, you can't imagine why your lover would be anything but honest and open with you at all times – manipulation just isn't your style.

If someone does break your heart, your grief is real and raw but, because you are able to express yourself so sincerely, you are able to process your emotions more quickly than the other zodiac signs. Phew!

WARRIOR SPIRIT

Ultimately, you are a fighter and you won't give up on love because you know you deserve it, and your self-belief demands it. You may experience your fair share of romances and break-ups but that's because you're a tougher cookie than most – the universe knows you can handle it. You may have something of an epic frog-kissing journey to complete before finding your prince or princess, but where's the challenge in finding your true love straight away? You're not one to dwell on past hurts, and eventually see them as milestones on the road as you battle your way to victory in love.

Most compatible
love signs

Aries – you love a challenge and only another Aries can handle your lava-hot passion without getting burned.

Leo – you're both enthusiastic and energetic. Leos need to be admired which you're happy to do, as long as they don't mind you bossing them around.

Libra – you're not intimidated by anyone, but there's something mysterious and magnetically appealing about your opposite sign of Libra.

Least compatible
love signs

Virgo – won't make love until the house is tidy and they've watched the news.

Taurus – dislikes being rushed and doesn't like being uncomfortable, which rules out your spontaneous desire to make love on the washing machine.

Cancer – you just plain scare Cancerians, who need to feel safe, secure and well understood before anyone is allowed get close. You don't have time for that!

Aries at work

*Y*ou love to lead, and you play to win – skills that can make you a legendary boss, and ultimately that's where you're heading! But to become top banana, you also need to master a few important workplace habits and skills.

You tend to throw yourself into the deep end, or enthusiastically plunge into new projects without wasting time, which is all very commendable and your boss will appreciate your energy. But a little more preparation will go a long way to help when you get stuck, or bored.

Be honest, you assume that thinking things through is just a delay tactic and that you'll fix any problems along the way. But a lack of foresight will cost you time, energy and probably money, further down the line.

Learn some patience and impress everyone you're working with that you're not just a flash in the pan. Next time you have a great idea, think of what you are trying to achieve and how you will get there. Write up a plan on action, work out a budget and discuss it with people who know more about it than you do … they're thin on the ground, admittedly, but there must be someone!

WORK ON: TEAMWORK

Why do you have to work with others at all dammit! You can accomplish far more on your own … or so you think. And this may be true to an extent. But other people are a fact of life at work, and isolating yourself from them will probably just make you a bit unpopular, and more likely to be left out of the coffee round.

Let other colleagues know you're available and willing to contribute. See your work partners and teammates as a challenge to be mastered. Learn the art of compromise and discover how to work more flexibly. Nobody likes someone that pushes in and takes all the glory for themselves. Share your success and include your colleagues in your thinking. Then when you do bump into an obstacle or have to deal with a difficult person, you won't be doing it all on your own.

Working in a group is a skill in itself and one that you'll have to get better at if you want to get to the top. You're a bright spark but your super self-confidence can be a little overbearing. However, when your colleagues see how fast you learn, how willing you are to put yourself forward for challenging tasks, and – most importantly – that you can also be trusted, they'll admire your pluck, and will soon learn that you'll be an asset on their team.

TOP SKILLS

Your eagerness and boundless energy are admirable and will catch your boss's eye and keep you fresh in their mind. Not everyone is as keen as you are to take on difficult challenges at work, and your innovative ideas will prove popular. You're never stuck for an answer and are often the one to kick off brainstorming sessions.

You're also a very quick learner and absorb new information lightning fast. But sometimes it's wise to slow down a little. Make sure that your impatience isn't getting in the way of actually listening to what people want you to do.

When your employers trust that you will take on other people's opinions without argument, or can take criticism without stapling their tie to the desk, you'll be worth your weight in gold to any organisation. And when you do get to the top, which is inevitable, you can be the one calling the shots – and everything will fall into its natural astrological order.

Most compatible colleagues

Sagittarius – genial, creative and always full of good ideas – they make you look good.

Taurus – you need Taurus, who is easy to boss around, reliable, and thorough – all the things you're not!

Gemini – you're not hot on details but get on a Gemini's good side and they'll type, talk, look as though they're listening, organise the Christmas party and make tea all at the same time.

Least compatible colleagues

Capricorn – they want to be the boss too, but they're sneakier, or possibly even cleverer about it than you – and you're not keen on that.

Pisces – dreamy Pisces just doesn't have enough urgency about them for you to believe they're getting any work done.

Aries – serious competition here and you really admire their style, but there's no room at the top for two alpha Rams!

Perfect Aries Careers

Surgeon

Lion tamer

Demolition expert

Professional athlete

Ambulance driver

First Aid responder

Soldier

Pilot

Police officer

Firefighter

Aries
Work Ethic

ARIES DON'T GET
SCARED WHEN
FACED WITH A
CHALLENGE ... THEY
GET EXCITED!

Aries friends and family

*Y*ou're a fun and exciting friend with bags of energy. You're rarely still and because you get bored so easily, you usually have new hobbies and interests on the go. You prefer going out and doing something with your buddies, rather than sitting around talking. Hot air ballooning, watching motorcycle racing, zorbing and hiking might be stimulating activities for you, but not all your friends will be so active and energetic.

One of the things your friends love about you is that you stick up for them so readily. You're fiercely protective of the people you care about, which makes for a formidable enemy, so woe betide anyone brave enough to annoy any of your friends as they'll have you to deal with. You love a good argument, though you prefer to call them 'heated discussions' when you're debating with pals. They, however, may see this differently!

You prefer to keep things lively in your social life, so you usually have a wide circle of people you see on a regular basis. Your warmth and enthusiasm attract people from all sorts of backgrounds. You enjoy variety, although you're loyal to a handful of very close friends. You don't take offence when people disappear, as you understand too well that life is like that. But you do get very hurt if a friend betrays or lies to you. Breaking your trust is agonising for you because it's simply not in your character to treat people like that yourself.

FAMILY DYNAMICS

You like your home life to be noisy, fun and adventurous. Camping trips, mountaineering, athletics and the gym are family favourites. You don't relish the cooking, cleaning and general upkeep of your home, but there's never a dull moment. Besides, who cares about the washing-up when there's a cabaret happening in the lounge, a zoo in the kitchen, and the family Olympic games in the garden?

ARIES PARENT

You're an encouraging, proud parent who gives their children plenty of room to grow. In many ways you're actually a big kid yourself, so you have a real affinity with the little ones and love their curiosity. You share their wonder and have a beguiling innocence that kids adore. You're the parent that doesn't mind if your kids get their hands dirty or have mismatched socks and you actively encourage tree climbing, bug hotels and rough-and-tumble activities that daintier parents would shy away from. If somebody upsets your offspring, there's usually hell to pay and you think nothing of telling teachers and other kids' parents exactly what you think of them.

ARIES CHILD

Aries children are fiercely independent, courageous and self-assertive. They learn early how to stick up for themselves and can sometimes be quite aggressive. Mars-ruled kids aren't particularly sulky, but they can have quite explosive tempers and they'll need plenty of exercise and activities to help them work through their high emotions. Aries kids can get fidgety if they're bored and they can be super-competitive at games. If you want to entertain an Aries child, tell them they can't do something and watch while they prove you wrong!

Healthy Aries

*T*he creative power of the Sun has bestowed you with a robust constitution and athletic abilities. You excel at games and sport and enjoy setting yourself goals and smashing through your targets. You're usually a fast mover but are more of a sprinter than a long-distance runner. You burn brightly but because you put so much energy in at the start, you can get exhausted. Ruled by energetic Mars, you put everything into your efforts but run out of patience if things get too samey. You like to change the scenery and to keep your goals interesting. Just changing your daily commute, or the grocery shop run, can give you a bit of a lift.

ACTIVITIES AND RELAXATION

Boxing, trampolining, hot yoga and running would all be excellent activities for your boisterous sign. You're no couch potato and need to keep yourself busy. Netflix every night would have you, quite literally, climbing the walls (another great activity for you).

You need space around you and plenty of fresh air – and you're not fussed if the weather's bad. Exercising in snow, wind and rain just adds to the challenge for you.

You're not usually a team player, preferring the freedom of going it alone, but it's different if we're talking about sport. You excel at any physically demanding team sports and are usually a key player.

Most other zodiac signs just can't match you on physical prowess, and eventually even you can't sustain your cheetah-like pace indefinitely. Because you use up so much energy, it's super-important that you match the energy out with energy back in and get plenty of sleep. You're more of a morning person than a night owl, and early nights will refresh your depleted batteries.

FOOD AND DRINK

You have a very healthy appetite and burn calories fast. As a Fire sign you enjoy hot, spicy food and are not a particularly fussy eater. Fast food works for you – as long as you balance it up with enough lively activity. If you could, you'd eat out at a different place every day. You don't always have the patience to cook and the thought of sampling new cuisines is too tempting to miss out on. You're more of a street food fan than a leisurely candlelit dinner person, and you prefer to grab and go and have a soft spot for carveries and buffets.

Red meat, hot peppers and curries are Aries foods and you have a penchant for energy drinks. You're not moved by bland tastes – the stronger the better you like it, but go easy on the caffeine and the coffee. You, more than most, need to switch off before going to bed. Everyone should drink plenty of water, but you should really take this to heart as Fire signs tend to burn their liquids quicker than most, so don't get dehydrated.

BODY AREA: HEAD

The Aries body area is the head and you may attract more than your fair share of headaches, tooth issues or sinusitis. The Sun's cosmic energy highlights your skull and face, which often manifests physically as red hair or as a strong pair of eyebrows!

Aries on the move

*Y*ou want an authentic experience of new places. You're not a tourist, you're a pioneer! You thrive in environments that have some of the other signs quaking in their boots. You rarely visit the same place twice and on vacation you're the person that fills every day of your stay with experiences. You're the last person to sit by the pool with a good book or not venture any further than the hotel bar. You need drama and amusement to keep you feeling alive and vital; that's what allows you to express yourself as freely as possible.

DESIGNATED SENSIBLE PERSON

You prefer to travel alone as companions may hold you back, which would just test your patience too much. You'd be pretty miserable on a museum or art gallery tour with friends or family who want to spend time examining every exhibit.

However, left to your own devices, can you really trust yourself with your hard-earned resources? Your impulsive streak could get you into some hot water and you're likely to get overexcited and just throw caution to the wind. Who wants to check their bank account or make sure they have a bed for the night when you're going tornado chasing or plane-wing walking?

You can be a little bit reckless sometimes and quickly run out of funds when you're having the time of your life. If you do plan to go away with a companion, perhaps a more frugal Capricorn or an organised Virgo would be a real asset. These more sensible earth-ruled types may steer you away from temptation and encourage you to sleep in a bed every now and then.

PERFECT TRIP

As the zodiac's tough guys and gals, backpacking, camping and hiking appeal to your love of the great outdoors and your independent nature. You're not worried about going without the little luxuries that more refined signs can't live without. Who needs hot water, electricity and clean clothes when you're hacking your way through the jungle barefoot in Thailand, or skiing over the frozen Canadian Tundra?

You're certainly not your average package holiday type of character. You'd rather plan as little as possible, just leaving home with a toothbrush, torch and a bundle of cash. You'll work it all out on the way. But even a tiny amount of organising could make the difference between a disaster and a fantastic adventure. Research where you're going – at least find out if your passport or visa needs updating. Many Aries have arrived at the airport before even thinking about whether they're actually allowed to go where they please. Laborious details such as vaccinations and respecting local dress codes and customs can come as a shock.

You lean towards lesser-known places and unique experiences you can make your own. Undiscovered islands, difficult terrain or exciting cities where you can be as brash, bold and as boisterous as you please. Large-scale sporting events hold some appeal too, especially if it's something you've not seen before. Even better if you can try your hand at whatever's on offer. Throw in some extreme sports such as bungee jumping or white-water rafting and we're looking at your perfect trip.

Aries
Favourite Places

Mountain top

Racetrack

Bangkok

Texas

Athletics stadium

Tent

Yellowstone Park

Aries
Travel Ethic

ADVENTURE IS
AT THE HEART OF
EVERY ARIES TRIP
– BORING DETAILS
CAN WAIT!

Aries
BIRTHDATE
PERSONALITIES

Discover your personal forecast for the day of your birth.

21 March

*Y*ou are a lively person who communicates passionately. Your sharp mind can be used to solve practical problems and you are very quick to learn but consequently can easily get bored. You are always ready for action, adaptable and highly versatile, and will take up any challenge offered. A natural debater, you think on your feet and have a ready wit. However, you do have a tendency – on many an occasion – to speak first and think later, which can lead to a reputation for being outspoken and slightly insensitive. Your mind works so fast you tend to interrupt others – which they can find annoying. Never fire off an email or text if upset or angry – wait to cool down. Divert yourself with a sport or martial art that needs mental agility, or you could try gentle, stress-reducing tai chi.

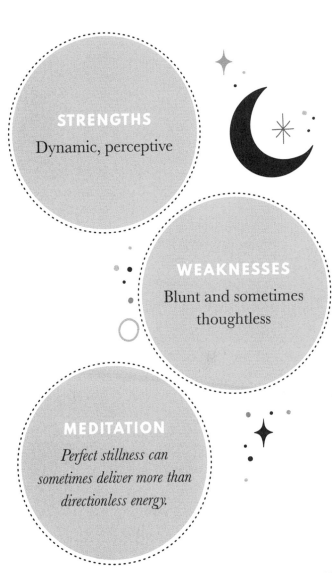

STRENGTHS

Dynamic, perceptive

WEAKNESSES

Blunt and sometimes thoughtless

MEDITATION

Perfect stillness can sometimes deliver more than directionless energy.

22 March

Y ou are a highly emotional and sensitive person who can become moody and cantankerous when upset. You are fiercely protective of the things in your life that you care about, especially your family and home, and will defend them at all costs. You are brilliant at sensing the public mood and can absorb others' feelings like a sponge. You can be overly concerned with what people feel about you – remember not to take things personally. Always on the go, you can easily burn out. You love fast food – it was invented for you! However, you need to ensure you never eat while upset. You love to keep everyone happy so can take on too many things. Ask for time to reflect before committing to projects, to make sure you really want to do them. Channel your energies into home improvements.

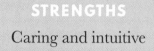

STRENGTHS

Caring and intuitive

WEAKNESSES

Moody, prone to emotional outbursts

MEDITATION

When we are helping others, we are nourishing the soul.

23 March

*Y*ou are a theatrical, big personality, with a strong desire to compete and win. You love being in the limelight, and radiate confidence and self-assurance. You appreciate honesty and directness and can't stand deceit. You are not known for your subtlety or finesse. You are always coming up with creative projects where you can take the leadership role. You take risks, will speculate and gamble. You have the willpower to succeed when others give up. You have courage and strength and boundless enthusiasm. As a natural leader with masses of physical energy, you need to acknowledge the contribution of others. You can be a workaholic and find it hard to delegate. Amateur dramatics, or solo sports, such as tennis, where you excel, will bring you satisfaction. The car you drive must reflect your sense of glamour.

STRENGTHS

Inspired, passionate

WEAKNESSES

Egotistical, slightly stubborn

MEDITATION

To conquer oneself is more of a challenge than conquering others.

24 March

*Y*ou are a productive and busy person who thrives on handling a variety of projects at once. You use up a lot of nervous energy which can cause inner tension and headaches. Your need to get things right is strong, which is great when dealing with written communication and editing. Excellent at detailed work with your hands, you are a natural craftsperson or artisan. You love to design systems and enjoy complex and demanding mental tasks. You want others to do things your way – the right way! You worry that what you produce isn't up to your high standards and this can produce negative energies, so working to a deadline helps you finish. When feeling mentally overwhelmed, time is well spent in decluttering and reorganising your work and living space.

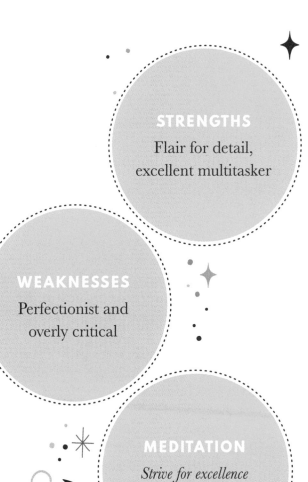

STRENGTHS

Flair for detail,
excellent multitasker

WEAKNESSES

Perfectionist and
overly critical

MEDITATION

*Strive for excellence
not perfection.*

25 March

*Y*ou are a charming, gregarious person who needs a life partner to find out who you are. They can bring out the best in you. A born romantic – and a bit of a flirt – you are highly creative and love the idea of love. Your heart can rule your head and you constantly need to be appreciated. You act confidently but can be rocked by the mildest negative comment. Your critics say you are self-centred, but those who know you appreciate how kindhearted you really are. You have a childlike creativity that touches people's hearts. Your heroism can be an inspiration. However, your tendency to emotionally see-saw can have you reaching for wine or chocolate as comfort – that's when you need to call friends over to talk things through instead of battling through it alone.

STRENGTHS
Endearing and sociable

WEAKNESSES
Indecisive, too eager
to please

MEDITATION
*Compare yourself
only to yourself.*

26 March

*Y*ou are a hypnotic and powerful person with magnetic appeal. You are unstoppable and once you set your mind on something you make sure you get it, by whatever means. You push yourself to the limits. You have a sharp mind and a sardonic sense of humour which serves to balance the underlying determination of your actions. People admire your courage as you are gracious in defeat, but you always come back to fight another day. There is a refreshing honesty in what you say; you tell it how it is. Some call this brutal, others love your frankness. In relationships and work, once you commit, you are in it for the duration. You are a passionate lover. To relax you need to let off steam; strengthening exercises – such as weightlifting or digging up the garden – are excellent.

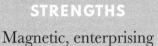

STRENGTHS
Magnetic, enterprising

WEAKNESSES
Ruthless and
brutally honest

MEDITATION
*A truth with a nasty intent
is worse than a lie.*

27 March

*Y*ou are larger than life, an adventurer who travels far in many ways. You are highly intuitive, very friendly and warm-hearted but can occasionally be highly strung and impatient with others who do not share your ideals. You have an intense moral certainty. A born philosopher and talker, you can speak for hours when campaigning about your pet cause. You have strong entrepreneurial skills. A big personality with fire in your belly, you can motivate others. When you're in love, you give yourself wholeheartedly. You suffer badly if let down, because rarely do you anticipate this possibility. Heal your wounds by escaping to the great outdoors; you'd enjoy going on safari or a camping trip to somewhere exotic and hot. Adventure re-inspires you and restores your high spirits.

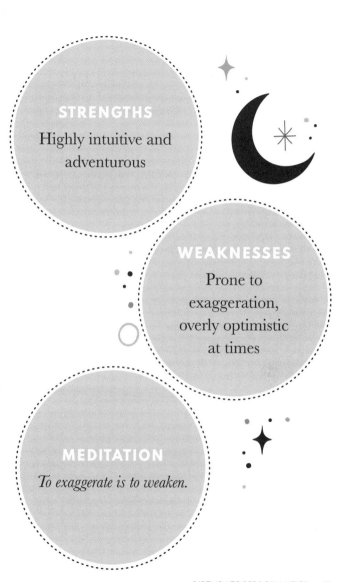

STRENGTHS

Highly intuitive and adventurous

WEAKNESSES

Prone to exaggeration, overly optimistic at times

MEDITATION

To exaggerate is to weaken.

28 March

*Y*ou are a tough-minded individual with a droll sense of humour. You are the boss, a realist who approaches life as a series of challenges to be conquered. You are a creative entrepreneur with ideas that are grounded and have longevity. You have talents that work well in the political arena. You respect those who have the audacity to teach you something new. In love you need to let your hair down and relax more; thinking about your job outside working hours is guaranteed to get under the skin of your partner. You are thick-skinned, so partners learn quickly that you respond best to straight talking. Take short breaks in the course of your working day, enjoy simple pleasures: eat an ice cream, walk barefoot on the grass. Remembering your inner child will rejuvenate you.

STRENGTHS
Droll sense of humour,
creative entrepreneur

WEAKNESSES
Workaholic, uptight

MEDITATION
*How beautiful it is to do
nothing, and then to rest
afterwards.*

29 March

You are an extremely friendly and sociable person with a passion for justice and human rights. Your leadership abilities combined with your progressive ways of thinking make you a natural campaigner for social causes. You are a rebel who does things their way. You have the capacity for being very successful because you possess a sharp intellect as well as charisma and a gift for persuasion. You should never be underestimated. Yours is a different vision for the world and others sit up and take note when you speak of it. You love to be with a group so relationships come naturally to you. You need intellectual stimulation with your partner and a lot of personal space. You run on nervous energy, so need to de-stress with some form of yoga – experiment until you find what suits you.

STRENGTHS

Gift of the gab,
friendly

WEAKNESSES

Over rational,
easily bored

MEDITATION

Blessed are the flexible,
for they shall not be
bent out of shape.

30 March

*Y*ou are a born optimist and your joie de vivre lights up a room when you enter. You have a strong inner core, and you know what you want, but can be easily distracted with too many irons in the fire. Your gifts are many and your versatility is your asset – and this is the reason people like you – you can relate. You have musical talent and can easily imitate others – you have an ear for the latest slang. Your energetic approach can wear others out and because you speak so fast some can find you too abrupt. Learning the art of pausing will serve you well. Your soulmate has to be someone who adores you and gives you the stability you need. You enjoy the cut and thrust of city life and your idea of relaxing is hanging out at a buzzing cafe or bar. Take time to watch and listen, so your ideas can focus.

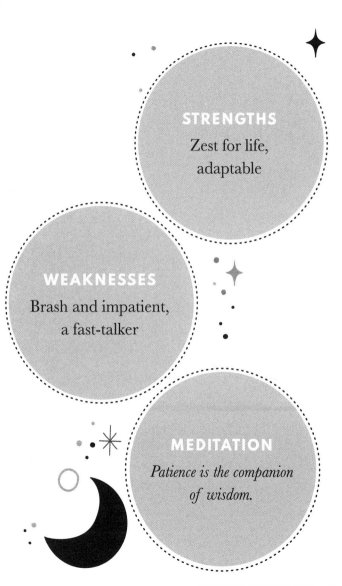

STRENGTHS

Zest for life,
adaptable

WEAKNESSES

Brash and impatient,
a fast-talker

MEDITATION

*Patience is the companion
of wisdom.*

31 March

*Y*ou are a natural carer and protector, with huge ambitions to do something positive for the planet. You can be daring and original with your ideas, taking them out into the world and never fretting about how others will perceive them. You have the ability to tune into what people need and will give it to them by saying exactly what they want to hear. You also have the drive to get things done. A secure family base is a necessity, providing a much-needed refuge after your travels. You can rush into things and fling yourself headfirst into projects without thought, then get upset when things don't turn out as you expected. If you swallow your feelings, your frustration can take its toll. Participating in team games for all the family – which have the element of fun rather than competition – is the answer.

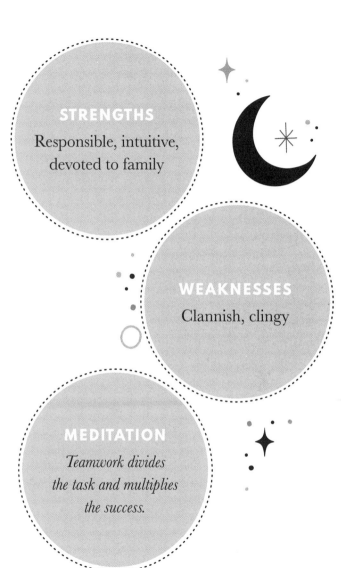

STRENGTHS
Responsible, intuitive, devoted to family

WEAKNESSES
Clannish, clingy

MEDITATION
Teamwork divides the task and multiplies the success.

1 April

*Y*ou are a one-off, a truly courageous person who leads the way with a pioneering spirit. You are prepared to risk everything, moving fast and without undue thought into uncharted territory. You are a true hero, never stopping to think of your own safety when your instincts tell you that someone or something needs your help. You have a forceful personality that people either love or loathe – you are not subtle! You can be very independent so a partnership can create difficulties. You can't bear to be number two. It works best if your partner has a life of their own, so when you do get together it's a honeymoon rather than a fight. You can burn out and neglect your body so your diet is of vital importance to keep your energy levels high. Remember that even the best-made engine needs an oil change!

STRENGTHS

Bold and heroic,
a pioneer and
individual

WEAKNESSES

Rash and impulsive
with a blunt approach

MEDITATION

*The trees that are slow
to grow bear the best fruit.*

2 April

*Y*ou are both gentle yet tough, diplomatic yet tactless. You are an enigma and very attractive to be with. You adore your romantic partners and they feel your admiration. You ooze a self-confidence which others envy. You love the material world and enjoy spending the considerable amount of money you can earn. You are determined to get what you want and you can rush in with undue haste which you regret later. Your sense of humour borders on the risqué, but you can get away with it if the occasion is right. You make an adorable companion and always have someone on your arm. A special relationship is essential for you, and two weeks alone has you climbing up the walls. You know how to take care of yourself. A good massage is essential for your peace of mind.

STRENGTHS

Self-assured, sexy

WEAKNESSES

Hasty, tactless

MEDITATION

Nature does not hurry,
yet everything is
accomplished.

3 April

*Y*ou are direct and very persuasive, you can sell anything to anybody. A natural comic, you come across as light and eternally youthful. You are constantly on the move and creative ideas flow from you. A notepad or dictaphone is an essential tool. You talk fast and people struggle to keep up with you. Your joie de vivre helps everybody feel more alive in your presence. You are a natural companion but get easily bored in relationships. You blow hot and cold and this is disconcerting for those of a steadier constitution. You have the gift of the gab, so be careful not to mislead others with false expectations. Keep your options open and don't make promises you can't keep. You can burn out with too much talking, so take time out to restore your energy by walking barefoot and grounding yourself.

STRENGTHS

Quick witted,
persuasive,
young at heart

WEAKNESSES

Short concentration
span, unpredictable

MEDITATION

*Silence is the true friend
that never betrays.*

4 April

*Y*our charisma appeals to all ages. An artist with a rich imagination, you have innate charm, with a natural flair in all you accomplish. You can stun people with your unique talents. Your creativity comes in fits and starts, and you can be unpredictable depending on how you feel about a project. Your sensitivity is both a blessing and a curse. When upset you sulk and nurse your wounds, but, like a child, you are ready to play the next day. In love, you are seeking to be mothered, and will test your partner to see if they care for you even when you throw a tantrum. You can get homesick and gain great comfort from childhood comforts – an old teddy bear or a home-made apple pie will make you feel rested once more. Once you learn to mother yourself, you'll be an excellent partner.

STRENGTHS

Charismatic, artistic flair, action-oriented

WEAKNESSES

Overemotional, moody and prone to self-pity

MEDITATION

Self-pity is self-destruction — think positive.

5 April

*Y*ou are a showman, a natural leader with an appetite for life. You know that you're the centre of the universe and it comes as no surprise that you have many admiring followers who want to know your secret. You are an inspiration to others by just being you. Innately warm and enthusiastic, you are a natural star who just has to shine. You can act like a prima donna and you do have a strong ego, so you need to take the leadership position or you will act like a child having a temper tantrum. You need passion and adoration from your partner and if they can help promote your career, all the better. Whatever you do, you need applause, so make sure you use your creativity and natural acting ability to entertain others. Your playfulness will always win them over in the end.

STRENGTHS

Generosity of spirit,
contagious enthusiasm

WEAKNESSES

Emotionally immature,
vain

MEDITATION

*The only cure for vanity
is laughter.*

6 April

You are straightforward and direct in your approach to life, yet there's an undercurrent of timidity and shyness. You have an ability to focus on the smallest thing and can be obsessive if everything isn't up to your exacting standards. At times you let loose and live life on a grand scale, but there is always a nagging inner critic highlighting your imperfections and holding you back. You can be too hard on yourself at times and need to learn to overlook mistakes in yourself and others. In romance you can veer between an almost Neanderthal approach and appearing to be so shy and retiring you lose out completely. When you get trapped in being too obsessive, try doing something that requires precision and shows off your talent for eye and hand coordination, such as needlework or playing snooker.

STRENGTHS
Modest, orderly

WEAKNESSES
Obsessive and timid

MEDITATION
*Whether you
think you can or
you think you can't,
you are right.*

7 April

*Y*ou are eager for life, a passionate person with an enthusiasm that is endearing yet tinged with emotional naivety. You are a lover, who needs a romantic lead to play opposite you. As an idealist, you seek the truth, but can often argue for an opposing view just to create lively debate and get people stirred up! You are prone to jealousy and this leads to fights with your lover. However, for you, anger is a form of foreplay which leads to the pleasure of making up, but be aware that this way of behaving can be difficult for a lover to cope with. Nevertheless a committed relationship would be the making of you. Once you master your emotions you are a born leader, skilled in the art of diplomacy. Vigorous physical activity – such as a good workout at the gym – is the best release when your temper gets too hot.

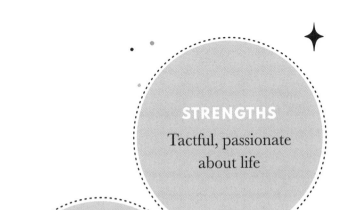

STRENGTHS

Tactful, passionate
about life

WEAKNESSES

Emotionally reserved,
insecure

MEDITATION

In jealousy there is more of
self-love than love.

8 April

*Y*ou are a charismatic, intense person and are on this Earth to make a statement with your life. You believe in your own abilities and your inner core is strong and resourceful. Whatever life throws up, you can survive; crises are the making of you. You have a penchant for investigating the dark side of life. While mainly quietly purposeful, you can be overly dramatic and come on too strong. You care what people think of you and need their approval, so cooling down your approach is necessary if you want to win them over. You need a strong partner to match you. Once you have found them you make a formidable team. You have enormous powers of endurance. Hard physical exercise – such as rowing or hitting the dancefloor with a strenuous routine – helps you release excess energy.

STRENGTHS
Resolute, captivating

WEAKNESSES
Overbearing with a
tendency to overreact

MEDITATION
*No one can whistle
a symphony — it takes
a whole orchestra
to play it.*

9 April

*Y*ou are a visionary with a large appetite for life. You see the big picture and your schemes are on the grand scale but the details bore you. Your enjoyment of life comes before anything else, and you are quite likely to drop everything and hop on a plane just for the fun of it. You are resilient and can easily handle setbacks – they are just challenges for you to overcome with innovative solutions. You are competitive and can wield a powerful influence over others. Love is a grand affair and you relish the experience of falling in love, which you do often – essentially you are in love with life and everything and everybody it has to offer. When someone puts a dampener on one of your ideas, you need to get to higher ground. This you can do literally – hot air ballooning or sky-diving was made for you.

STRENGTHS
Fun loving and resilient

WEAKNESSES
Lack of attention
to detail, restless

MEDITATION
*The greatest glory
is not in never falling,
but in rising every
time we fall.*

10 April

*Y*ou are a determined person with a forceful manner. You possess considerable flair and a talent for organising. You are ambitious from a young age and set your sights high. You are a winner, and although you respect tradition you can shock people out of their stagnant ways. You have a wicked sense of humour, a scathing wit and can use sarcasm to get your point across. You do what you say you're going to do, which is refreshing in the modern world. You choose your life partner with the same common-sense approach you have to your work. Love is a business partnership and you value the marriage contract highly. When your head is fit for bursting, you need to let go of the responsible you and do something silly. Watch a movie just for the fun of it – a Disney classic is perfect.

STRENGTHS
Determined, with great management skills

WEAKNESSES
Emotionally restrained, solemn

MEDITATION
Cultivate your sense of humour — laughter is the best medicine.

11 April

*Y*ou are full of bright ideas and a real people person. You have an offbeat way of looking at the world. You can express your controversial views with such passion that people pull back, then they hear what you have to say and become fervent supporters. Routine bores you and you're not great at finishing what you've started. You thrive on change. You are best being self-employed and will work long into the night if the inspiration takes you. You are an anarchist and can find your niche in the media, fashion or film industries where you can express your originality. In romantic relationships you are looking for a friend first, a lover second. Your ideal partner keeps you guessing as well as being your best companion. You would do well to combine physical exercise with having fun, so frisbee was invented for you.

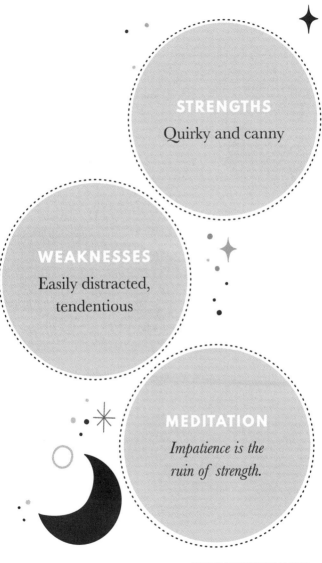

STRENGTHS
Quirky and canny

WEAKNESSES
Easily distracted,
tendentious

MEDITATION
*Impatience is the
ruin of strength.*

12 April

You are a paradox: brave and single-minded, but quaking with doubt inside. You can run the show or give in to the feelings of others and shrink from the excessive exposure that the spotlight brings, drifting off into your own dream world. But you have a fertile imagination and this needs to be channelled into artistic creations. Your feelings have to be expressed and putting them down on paper is essential for your growth. You can be too easily influenced by others and give up your personal ambitions or go into sacrifice mode. In relationships you need a partner who nurtures and supports you and gives you space to follow your dreams. When you are feeling out of balance and in need of inspiration, take to the water, either sailing or swimming – even a long shower will nourish your soul.

STRENGTHS

Ingenious, courageous

WEAKNESSES

Self-contradicting, emotionally impressionable

MEDITATION

A strong person and a waterfall always channel their own path.

13 April

*Y*ou are a man or woman who can act as a spokesperson for people who can't stand up for themselves. You understand how others feel, and can express empathy by taking a stance on behalf of the underdog. Your compassionate nature appeals to both the heads and hearts of others and this quality brings you the friendship of people from all walks of life. Nevertheless, you are a complex, volatile person and you create many dramas in your personal life. If you find people steering clear of you, you can bet you've gone too far. When you're feeling strong you assert yourself and command the stage of your life with supreme confidence. Your relationship is your rock and truly assists you in advancing your career. When you're depressed, a steam bath or sauna can do wonders to revitalise you.

STRENGTHS

Empathetic and
warm-hearted

WEAKNESSES

Temperamental,
with a tendency to
overdramatise

MEDITATION

*Never write a letter
while you are angry.*

14 April

*Y*our noble manner and integrity have been part of who you are since childhood. You have a social magnetism that exudes vitality. People respect you and want to be in your inner circle. Your intensity, deep convictions, warmth and intelligence are the ingredients to your success in life. Your streak of 'devil may care' can lead you to risk all for love and romance. For your relationships to work, you need to have respect for your partner. You have very high standards – only the best will do. If your pride is hurt or you are ignored, you suffer loudly and march off. This can lead you to extravagance, and indulgence in retail therapy on a grand scale. If you really need some pampering and to be made to feel special, having a facial or a great haircut might be easier on the wallet.

STRENGTHS
Honourable with great reverence for others

WEAKNESSES
Self-important and wasteful

MEDITATION
A bargain is only a bargain if it is something you need.

15 April

*Y*ou are outspoken and have clear ideas of how things should be done. You get impatient if you aren't at the centre of any action, with you taking the leading role. You are dutiful and highly disciplined, especially when it comes to performing daily tasks. You love routine yet long to break free and throw caution to the wind. You can be reckless one minute and then overly careful and cautious the next. Learning to trust yourself and others can enable you to be carefree – and that is your ultimate goal. You are creative and you get great satisfaction from a job well done. In affairs of the heart, you desire excitement and adventure and are torn between settling down and playing the field. Your tendency to self-doubt can give you sleepless nights, so a warm bath and lavender can help you to relax.

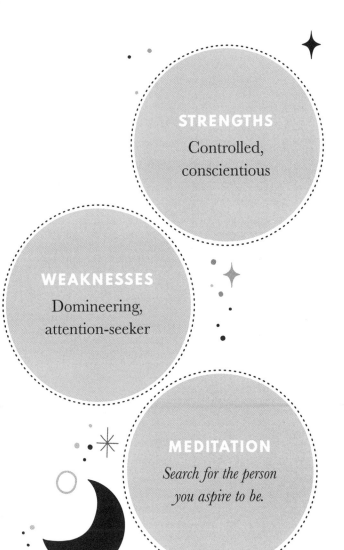

STRENGTHS
Controlled,
conscientious

WEAKNESSES
Domineering,
attention-seeker

MEDITATION
*Search for the person
you aspire to be.*

16 April

*Y*ou are a forthright, impulsive person who wears their heart on their sleeve. In every relationship you come up against the question, who's in charge, them or me? This is due to the delicate balancing act you perform in your life. The courage you have to bounce back after a heartbreak is admirable; in this respect you are a hero and your life is spent seeking the fairy-tale ending. You need a partner who loves adventure and excitement, someone who enjoys the highs and lows of the drama that is your life. Teamwork gives you the support you need and helps to put you in the spotlight where you belong. You need to learn to express your feelings when hurt – a close friend can help heal your tender heart. Never eat when upset, you are more sensitive than you let on.

STRENGTHS

Courageous,
determined

WEAKNESSES

Emotionally naive and
confrontational

MEDITATION

*The walls we build
keep out the joy as well as
the sadness.*

17 April

You embody a range of admirable qualities being highly motivated, ambitious and tenacious. Your powers of persuasion are endearing. You show sincerity and integrity once you are on your chosen path. You excel in the world of theatre or sport where your powerfully dramatic style comes into its own. You can be underhanded and play a political game which can embroil you in conflicts and leave you wondering why friends have turned on you. This can result in self-doubt. Recognise that you have the ability to transform your life and begin anew. A strong relationship is your biggest asset. You are faithful unless betrayed. When angry it's best to relieve your tension by boxing a punchbag or pillow rather than getting into a shouting match with your sweetheart.

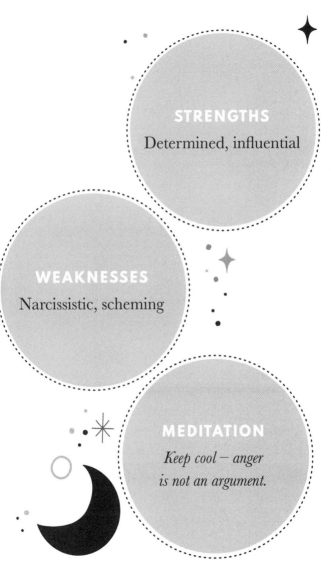

STRENGTHS

Determined, influential

WEAKNESSES

Narcissistic, scheming

MEDITATION

*Keep cool — anger
is not an argument.*

18 April

*Y*ou are spontaneous and here to enjoy life. You are ardent and passionate and love to gamble – you will risk all for what you believe in. Foreign cultures excite you, and you are keen to explore different religions. You always see the good in people and are unaware of the flaws in some of your enterprises. Your optimism is contagious and people love your openness and childlike trust in life. You are gregarious and in all your relationships you are uncomplicated, and direct. A partner needs to understand that you require freedom and space to do your own thing. At times you can verge on being bawdy which surprises your more delicate colleagues. In an argument you feel you are right, which results in a showdown. Back off and ask the question, do you want to be right or happy?

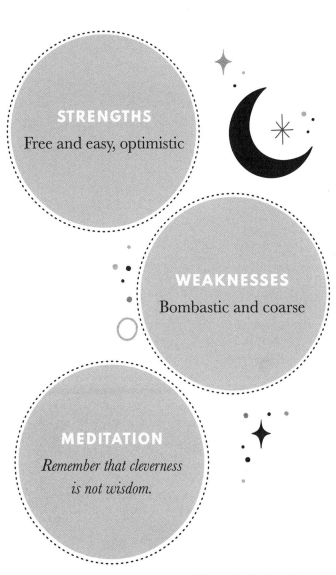

STRENGTHS
Free and easy, optimistic

WEAKNESSES
Bombastic and coarse

MEDITATION
*Remember that cleverness
is not wisdom.*

19 April

*Y*ou are a real go-getter, a person with a certain cheekiness that comes out of the blue as you can adopt a serious manner on first meeting. You are prodigious in your output, and your work is your life. You are devoted to truth and can get quite arrogant if someone dares to challenge your belief. Although you make fun of the establishment, you respect the law. You are unwavering in your rise to the top, and you get there – however long it takes you. You have an essentially practical way of looking at life with an earthiness that people respect. When you fall in love it is with a passion that takes your beloved by surprise. Commitment is second nature for you, so you can marry young but to an older person. Unwind by exploring the child's world of play: build sandcastles and swim with dolphins.

STRENGTHS
Cheeky, fun-loving
and unpretentious

WEAKNESSES
Strident, arrogant

MEDITATION
Smile when it hurts most.

20 April

*Y*ou have a flair for living, with a strong sensuality and magnetic appeal to both men and women. In public life you are dominant, yet in private you are yielding and soft. You possess formidable drive and energy that can be overwhelming for some. If you don't want to do something no one can persuade you, you just dig your heels in. You enjoy your successes, you know you deserve them. You never like to be taken for granted by your lover and are possessive and prone to jealousy, maybe due to your own roving eye. You can brood if you're ignored and sometimes you find it hard to throw off your moods. Once you get going again – a splendid meal and a glass of wine helps – you are irresistible once more. If that fails, a good night's sleep always works to restore your bonhomie.

STRENGTHS

Sensual, with an electrifying magnetism

WEAKNESSES

Insecure and stubborn

MEDITATION

Concentrate the mind on the present moment.

Going
DEEPER

Astrology has
more to give than just
your Sun sign ... learn to
read the complexities
in your personal
birth chart.

Your personal birth chart

*U*nderstanding your Sun sign is an essential part of astrology, but it's the tip of the iceberg. To take your astrological wisdom to the next level, you'll need a copy of your own unique birth chart – a map of the heavens for the precise moment you were born. You can find your birth chart at the Free Horoscopes link at: www.astro.com.

ASTROLOGICAL SYNTHESIS

When you first explore your chart, you'll find that as well as a Sun sign, you also have a Moon sign, plus a Mercury, Venus, Mars, Jupiter, Saturn, Neptune, Uranus and Pluto sign – and that they all mean something different. Then there's astrological houses to consider, ruling planets and Rising signs, aspects and element types – all of which you will learn more about in the section Birth Charts on pages 112–115.

The art to astrology is in synthesising all this intriguing information to paint a picture of someone's character, layer by layer. Now that you understand your Aries Sun character better, it's time to go deeper, and to look at the next layer – your Moon sign. To find your own Moon sign go to pages 104–111.

THE MOON'S INFLUENCE

After the Sun, your Moon sign is the second biggest astrological influence in your birth chart. It describes your emotional nature – your feelings, instincts and moods and how you respond to different sorts of people and situations. By blending your outer, Aries Sun character with your inner, emotional, Moon sign, you'll get a much more balanced picture of your whole personality. If you don't feel that you're 100% Aries, your Moon sign will explain why.

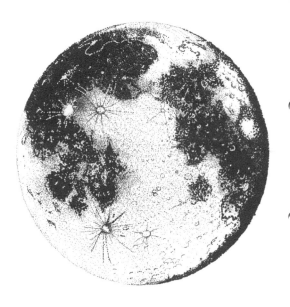

Aries with Moon signs

ARIES SUN/**ARIES MOON**

You are a dynamic, independent and self-confident person born on a new Moon. You can get impatient with people and can be quite demanding in your relationships because you tend to gloss over difficult feelings. Ignoring your emotions can lead to the occasional angry outburst, where you're not entirely sure where the energy is coming from. Plenty of physical activity and rest will help you keep on an even keel. You have phenomenal leadership skills and are quite fearless, even intimidating. Your double Mars ruling planets mean your instinct is to charge headlong into any new situation. But you've probably already learned that a more measured approach usually works better for yourself – and everyone else. On the outside you may appear tough, but you're much more easily hurt than you'd admit. And you're certainly not going to let anyone see your vulnerable side.

ARIES SUN/**TAURUS MOON**

Your Taurus Moon tempers your fiery nature, lending you more patience and making you more resilient. Your Mars/

Venus ruling planets demand the best quality from food, music and clothing. You may have an excellent singing voice, or certainly a noticeable one, as Taurus governs the neck area and Aries rules the head. The Aries in you relies on Taurus for keeping your feet on the ground and for finishing things you start. You have guts, determination and the willpower to take you to the top of your career. You're not strong on finessing the details and you're happy with a 'no frills' approach to life but your Venus-ruled Moon tempers your raw Aries Sun with tact and social skills.

ARIES SUN/**GEMINI MOON**

 If you're an Aries/Gemini mix you're a dextrous, clever clogs with ever-changing moods. Your Mars-ruled dominating Sun energy is channelled through your chatty Mercury-ruled emotional centre. This can mean you have a tendency to over-intellectualise your emotions, rather than just feeling them. You're happy to talk about your feelings but you're not that comfortable actually experiencing them. You tend to talk through your decisions with other people rather than analysing the options on your own. You often speak before you think and jump to conclusions. But your Mercury-ruled Moon learns fast from your experiences, encouraging you to consider your thoughts more carefully. You are spookily good at knowing how other people are feeling – often better than you are at judging your own emotional state.

ARIES SUN/**CANCER MOON**

Your Moon-ruled Cancer Moon sign gives you heaps of emotional intelligence and insight, which can get a little side-tracked by your fiery Sun sign. Perhaps you don't take your feelings as seriously as you should, or you may just prefer to keep them locked up. But eventually they'll need expression and will erupt like a volcano if ignored for too long. Your Moon/Mars powers have tremendous capacity for endurance and empathy, which could mean you are more forgiving of others' foibles than most. But your Aries Sun won't let anyone take advantage of you, and that tough Mars energy will eventually rise to the surface. On first meeting you, nobody would realise what a softy you really are, and that's how you like it to be.

ARIES SUN/**LEO MOON**

This is a very warm and generous combination, as both are Fire elements and therefore very compatible. Your Mars Sun blended with a Sun-ruled Moon is a harmonious, energetic and fun-loving combination. You have a big heart and like to express your feelings in dramatic fashion. You like being the centre of attention and you're probably a big hit at parties. Your full-on Fire energy can be a little bit much for quieter types, and you've probably learned the hard way that you can't please everyone all of the time. You're a creative and enthusiastic person, and a popular boss or leader. You are confident in your decisions, and you have a knack for making other people believe in you. Though you quickly lose interest if others don't share your enthusiasm.

ARIES SUN/**VIRGO MOON**

Your Mercury-ruled Virgo Moon sign can make you a very cool cat indeed. Your Mars-ruled Sun's tendencies to charge in and take control is tempered by a more modest and refined Mercury-ruled Virgo approach. When your head and heart are working together, you're one of the most effective people in the zodiac! Your Aries energy and drive to succeed is backed up by considerable intellectual power and earthy Virgo determination. You're not as forceful as your typical Aries, and your analytical Moon holds you back from jumping to conclusions or making rash decisions. Nobody can pull the wool over the eyes of a shrewd Mercury/Mars combo!

ARIES SUN/**LIBRA MOON**

Aries and Libra are opposite signs of the zodiac, which means you were born at a full Moon. Ruled by Mars and Venus respectively an Aries/Libra combination both compliments and pulls away from each other. Your Aries Sun wants to take decisive action and your Libra Moon calls for balance and consideration. Your Libra Moon instinctively seeks comfort in relationships, while your Aries Sun screams for independence and freedom. When blended together, each extreme either tempers the other – or emphasises the differences. Emotionally it's swings and roundabouts, and you learn from experience to balance these conflicting aspects of your personality. This ability to harmonise makes you excellent at reading a room because you instinctively understand how to be the go-between or middle ground, for wildly different types of people.

ARIES SUN/**SCORPIO MOON**

If you are a Mars-ruled person with a Pluto-ruled Scorpio Moon, your emotional nature is magnified. To the outside world, your Scorpio Moon may appear almost emotionless but that's because you're an expert at keeping your feelings to yourself. Your feelings run very deep and when matched with an Aries Sun, you are a force of nature. Aries Suns like to express themselves freely and impulsively, so when they're tempered by a secretive Scorpio Moon, there's a disconnect. Your emotional intelligence shines through, but it can be challenging to find the right people to take your feelings seriously. Your Aries Sun doesn't like to be held back by Scorpio's need to get under the surface, but when others appreciate that you're not all bluff and bluster, they'll keep you in their lives as long as possible.

ARIES SUN/**SAGITTARIUS MOON**

This double Fire blend of Mars-ruled Aries with Jupiter-ruled Sagittarius is an optimistic and enterprising blend. You don't believe in saying no to anything and have an unparalleled appetite for adventure. You're philosophical emotionally, wise and generous but you don't enjoy being held back. There's a whole world to explore and you're the person who wants to experience everything you can, wholeheartedly. All this love of excitement and learning can make it harder to deal with life's annoying details: earning enough money, looking after a family and eating properly. But your lesson in life is to do just that – find harmony between your lust for adventure without sacrificing the practicalities. And with all that enthusiasm and fire in your blood, you do this rather beautifully.

ARIES SUN/**CAPRICORN MOON**

Your Ram Sun sign blended with a Goat Moon sign makes for one persistent and ambitious person. Your Saturn-ruled Moon likes to do things thoroughly and slowly, with a mind on getting to the top. While your Aries Sun has the drive, energy and sheer self-belief to propel you there with force. Emotionally you can be a little shy and reserved but your Aries Sun means you are never cold or remote. Your earthy Moon is a little status-conscious and works hard to achieve all you value in life. This is fuelled by the fire of your Aries Sun, giving you the rocket fuel to achieve any dream. Your inner drive for success is unrivalled and your spontaneous Aries Sun means you'll enjoy life's pleasures along the way.

ARIES SUN/**AQUARIUS MOON**

This mix of Fire and Air makes you a sociable and magnetic character. Mars-ruled with innovative Uranus ruling your Moon means you need freedom and plenty of intellectual stimulation. You may not be entirely comfortable with your own emotional nature, as Aquarian Moons can be a little aloof, but your Aries Sun adds warmth and enthusiasm that draw people to you easily. Sometimes you are more comfortable when talking to friends than you are in a more intense one-to-one relationship. For this reason you may even prefer a more unconventional lifestyle, ditching a traditional family set-up or romantic relationship for a different way of life altogether. Your pioneering Aries Sun helps you feel happy with your eccentric choices – at least nobody can accuse you of being ordinary!

ARIES SUN/**PISCES MOON**

Your sensitive Neptune-ruled Pisces Moon is quite at odds with your outer, bolshier persona. You may lack a little confidence and you may find yourself making bold moves or statements only to backtrack later down the line. On an emotional level you are a deeply empathic and soul-searching individual which can be tricky when you just want to stamp your individuality on everything you do. Pisces Moons more than any other absorb the feelings of others, and Aries isn't used to taking everyone's feelings into account at all. But when it comes to art, music, writing or any creative endeavour, you'll be able to smash through any goals you set for yourself. Your Aries Sun can't resist a deadline!

Birth charts

*L*earning about your Sun and Moon sign opens the gateway into exploring your own birth chart. This snapshot of the skies at the moment of birth is as complex and interesting as the person it represents. Astrologers the world over have been studying their own birth charts and those of people they know, their whole lives and still find something new in them every day. There are many schools of astrology and an inexhaustible list of tools and techniques, but here are the essentials to get you started …

ZODIAC SIGNS AND PLANETS

These are the keywords for the 12 zodiac signs and the planets associated with them, known as ruling planets.

 ARIES
courageous, bold, aggressive, leading, impulsive

Ruling planet
 MARS
shows where you take action and how you channel your energy

TAURUS
reliable, artistic, practical, stubborn, patient

Ruling planet
VENUS
describes what you value and who and what you love

GEMINI
clever, friendly, superficial, versatile

Ruling planet
MERCURY
represents how your mind works and how you communicate

CANCER
emotional, nurturing, defensive, sensitive

Ruling planet
MOON
describes your emotional needs and how you wish to be nurtured

LEO
confidence, radiant, proud, vain, generous

Ruling planet
SUN
your core personality and character

VIRGO
analytical, organised, meticulous, thrifty

Ruling planet
MERCURY
co-ruler of Gemini and Virgo

LIBRA
fair, indecisive, cooperative, diplomatic

Ruling planet
VENUS
co-ruler of Taurus and Libra

SCORPIO
regenerating, magnetic, obsessive, penetrating

Ruling planet
PLUTO
deep transformation, endings and beginnings

SAGITTARIUS
optimistic, visionary, expansive, blunt, generous

Ruling planet
JUPITER
travel, education and faith in a higher power

CAPRICORN
ambitious, responsible, cautious, conventional

Ruling planet
SATURN
your ambitions, work ethic and restrictions

AQUARIUS
unconventional, independent, erratic, unpredictable

Ruling planet
URANUS
where you rebel or innovate

PISCES
dreamy, chaotic, compassionate, imaginative, idealistic

Ruling planet
NEPTUNE
your unconscious, and where you let things go

The 12 houses

irth charts are divided into 12 sections, known as houses, each relating to different areas of life as follows:

FIRST HOUSE
associated with *Aries*

Identity – how you appear to others, and your initial response to challenges

SECOND HOUSE
associated with *Taurus*

How you make and spend money, your talents, skills and how you value yourself

THIRD HOUSE
associated with *Gemini*

Siblings, neighbours, communication and short distance travel

FOURTH HOUSE
associated with *Cancer*

Home, family, your mother, roots and the past

FIFTH HOUSE
associated with *Leo*

Love affairs, romance, creativity, gambling and children

SIXTH HOUSE

6

associated with *Virgo*

Health, routines, organisation and pets

EIGHTH HOUSE

8

associated with *Scorpio*

Sex, death, transformation, wills and money you share with another

SEVENTH HOUSE

7

associated with *Libra*

Relationships, partnerships, others and enemies

NINTH HOUSE

9

associated with *Sagittarius*

Travel, education, religious beliefs, faith and generosity

TENTH HOUSE

10

associated with *Capricorn*

Career, fathers, ambitions, worldly success

ELEVENTH HOUSE

11

associated with *Aquarius*

Friends, groups, ideals and social or political movements

TWELFTH HOUSE

12

associated with *Pisces*

Spirituality, the unconscious mind, dreams and karma

THE ELEMENTS

Each zodiac sign belongs to one of the four elements – Earth, Air, Fire and Water – and these share similar characteristics, as listed below.

EARTH

Taurus, Virgo, Capricorn

Earth signs are practical, trustworthy, thorough and logical.

AIR

Gemini, Libra, Aquarius

Air signs are clever, flighty, intellectual and charming.

FIRE

Aries, Leo, Sagittarius

Fire signs are active, creative, warm, spontaneous, innovators.

WATER

Cancer, Scorpio, Pisces

Water signs are sensitive, empathic, dramatic and caring.

PLANETARY ASPECTS

The aspects are geometric patterns formed by the planets and represent different types of energy. They are usually shown in two ways – in a separate grid or aspect grid and as the criss-crossing lines on the chart itself. There are oodles of different aspect patterns, but to keep things simple we'll just be working with four: conjunctions, squares, oppositions and trines.

CONJUNCTION

0 degrees apart
intensifying

SQUARE

90 degrees apart
challenging

OPPOSITION

180 degrees apart
polarising

TRINE

120 degrees apart
harmonising

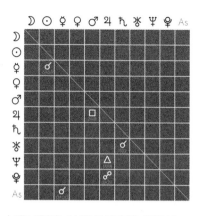

Planetary aspects for Katy's chart

HOUSES AND RISING SIGN

Each chart is a 360° circle, divided into 12 segments known as the houses (see pages 116–117 for house interpretations). The most important point in a birth chart is known as the Rising sign, also known as the Ascendant. This is usually shown as ASC or AS on the chart and it shows the zodiac sign that was rising on the Eastern horizon for the moment you were born. It's always on the middle left of the chart on the dividing line of the first house – the house associated with the self, how you appear to others, and the lens through which you view the world. The Rising sign is the position from where the other houses and zodiac signs are drawn in a counter-clockwise direction.

CHART RULER: The planetary ruler of a person's Rising zodiac sign is always a key player in unlocking a birth chart and obtaining a deeper understanding of it.

A SIMPLE BIRTH CHART INTERPRETATION FOR AN ARIES SUN PERSON

BIRTH CHART FOR KATY, BORN ON 14 APRIL 1988 IN LONDON AT 6.00AM

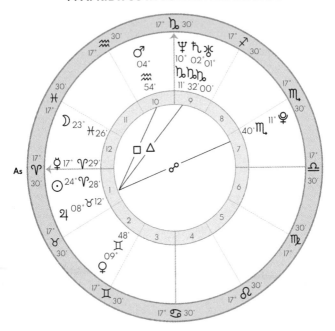

THE POSITIONS OF THE PLANETS: Katy has Aries Rising. You can see that her Sun is also in Aries, the Moon is in Pisces, Mercury is in Aries, Venus is in Gemini, Mars is in Aquarius, Jupiter occupies Taurus, Saturn, Uranus and Neptune are all in Capricorn and Pluto sits in Scorpio. Do also note the house positions that the planets are in.

INTERPRETATION BASICS

How do you begin to put all these signs and symbols together? It's usually best to begin with the Sun, Rising sign and chart ruler, and then to examine the condition of the Moon sign.

SUN, MOON, RISING SIGN AND CHART RULER: Katy's Sun and Rising sign (the way she approaches the world and how others see her) are both in Aries, which means she's a very strong-willed, enthusiastic person. Her Aries Sun is also in the first house, which is also strongly associated with Aries, so this further emphasises her passionate, physically energetic, Mars-ruled qualities. Because her Rising sign is Aries and is therefore ruled by Mars, Mars becomes her chart ruler. Katy's Mars sign is Aquarius in the tenth house of ambitions. Mars in Aquarius offers some balance to all that hot-headedness and shows aims connected with groups and social movements. Katy's Moon is in dreamy, ethereal Pisces, in the twelfth house, which is also connected with Pisces – which makes it doubly strong. Pisces Moons are very intuitive, artistic and sensitive, which she may hide beneath her bold Aries persona.

By looking at just these few points you immediately learn that the Sun sign's personality traits alone, although a crucial area of the chart, is often just one part of the person's overall picture.

OTHER PLANETS: Mercury (communication) is sitting right on her Rising sign and is in Aries. She's open, honest and direct, and she may even have a powerful voice. Jupiter (travel, optimism, overdoing things) is in comfort-loving Taurus, so we can assume she enjoys food, cooking and home comforts. Her Taurus Jupiter sits in her first house of identity, so she will be quite conscious of these qualities in herself.

Saturn, Uranus and Neptune all sit together (conjunction) in Capricorn, which is ambitious, determined and methodical. This chimes well with her tenth house (Capricorn-oriented) chart ruler Mars. However, these three planets all occupy the ninth house of travel and philosophy, so perhaps Katy dreams of travelling the world or is interested in different cultures and belief systems. Resourceful Pluto occupies Scorpio in her seventh house of partnerships. This position describes intense relationships and a dramatic love life.

ADDING IN THE PLANETARY ASPECTS

Let's take a brief look at the strongest aspects – the ones with the most exact angles or 'orbs' to the planetary degrees (the numbers next to the planets on the chart).

MERCURY CONJUNCTS SUN AND RISING SIGN: As noted above, this feisty conjunction adds yet more power and courage to her already heavily Aries-themed chart.

JUPITER SQUARES MARS: Katy has a very busy Jupiter! The square is a challenging aspect, but usually forces the person to grow – especially apt her as her Jupiter is in her first house of personality. Taurus loves luxury and is the sign of money, perhaps Katy needs to stick to a strict budget and beware of overindulging in food and drink.

JUPITER OPPOSES PLUTO: Oppositions show polarities – seesawing circumstances or conditions. With her Pluto in her partnership house, she may have a few rocky relationships before she finds the right person. Her choices of partner may be are quite literally 'opposed' by forces out of her control. Pluto in the seventh house can sometimes indicate a very powerful partnership.

JUPITER TRINE NEPTUNE: Trines are harmonious and are often skills so natural to us that we're not even aware of them. Katy's Jupiter/Neptune trine suggests she has great empathy interest in other cultures and people from a different background to hers.

URANUS CONJUNCT SATURN: Uranus (change and rebellion) and Saturn (structure and work ethic) are pushed together reinforcing their symbolism. Katy's ambitions or her career may dramatically change throughout her life. Her packed ninth house indicates a need for freedom and a dislike of being pigeonholed.

YOUR JOB AS AN ASTROLOGER

The interpretation above is simplified to help you understand some of the nuts and bolts of interpretation. Keep in mind when you're putting the whole thing together that astrology doesn't show negatives or positives. The planets represent potential and opportunities, rather than definitions set in stone. It's your job as an astrologer to use the planets' wisdom to blend and synthesise those energies to create a whole personality. It can take years to master the art of astrology but with these simple tools as your starting point, you'll discover it is an enlightening and fascinating process!

Going deeper

To see your own birth chart visit: www.astro.com and click the Free Horoscopes link and then enter your birth information. If you don't know what time you were born, put in 12.00pm. Your Rising sign and the houses might not be right, but the planets will be in the correct zodiac signs and the aspects will be accurate.

Further reading and credits

WWW.ASTRO.COM

This amazing astrological resource is extremely popular with both experienced and beginner astrologers. It's free to sign up and obtain your birth chart and personalised daily horoscopes.

BOOKS

PARKER'S ASTROLOGY by Derek and Julia Parker (Dorling Kindersley)

THE LITTLE BOOK OF ASTROLOGY by Marion Williamson (Summersdale)

THE BIRTHDAY ORACLE by Pam Carruthers (Arcturus)

THE 12 HOUSES by Howard Sasportas (London School of Astrology)

THE ARKANA DICTIONARY OF ASTROLOGY by Fred Gettings (Penguin)

THE ROUND ART by AJ Mann (Paper Tiger)

THE LUMINARIES by Liz Greene (Weiser)

SUN SIGNS by Linda Goodman (Pan Macmillan)

Marion Williamson is a best-selling astrology author and editor. *The Little Book of Astrology* and *The Little Book of the Zodiac* (Summersdale 2018) consistently feature in Amazon's top 20 astrology books. These were written to encourage beginners to move past Sun signs and delve into what can be a lifetime's study. Marion has been writing about different areas of self-discovery for over 30 years. A former editor of *Prediction* magazine for ten years, Marion had astrology columns in *TV Times*, *TV Easy*, *Practical Parenting*, *Essentials* and *Anglers Mail* for over ten years. Twitter: @_I_am_astrology

Pam Carruthers is a qualified professional Vedic and Western astrologer and student of *A Course in Miracles*. An experienced Life Coach and Trainer, Pam helps clients discover the hidden patterns that are holding them back in their lives. A consultation with her is a life-enhancing and healing experience. She facilitates a unique transformational workshop 'Healing your Birth Story' based on your birthchart. Based in the UK, Pam has an international clientele.

All images courtesy of Shutterstock and Freepik/ Flaticon.com.